A Passion for Books

TERRY W. GLASPEY

Harvest House Publishers
Eugene, Oregon

A Passion for Books

Published by Harvest House Publishers
Eugene, Oregon 97402

Library of Congress Cataloging-in-Publication Data
Glaspey, Terry W.
A passion for books / Terry W. Glaspey.
p. cm.
ISBN 1-56507-781-4
1. Books and reading. 2. Books and reading—Quotations, maxims, etc. I. Title.
Z1003.G52 1998
028'.9—dc21 98-12946
CIP

Design by Left Coast Design, Portland, Oregon

The author and Harvest House Publishers have made every effort to trace the ownership of all poems and quotes. In the event of a question arising from the use of any poem or quote, we regret any error made and will be pleased to make the necessary correction in future editions of this book.

Printed in the United States of America.

98 99 00 01 02 03 04 05 06 07 / IP / 10 9 8 7 6 5 4 3 2 1

CONTENTS

CHAPTER 1

A LOVE AFFAIR WITH BOOKS

I came late to a love for books.

Like most children of my generation, I spent countless hours in front of the television set, eyes glued to its latest offerings. Arriving home from school I would throw my coat and lunch box onto the couch and flip on the television set, always somewhat amazed as that hard little star of white light whined and then exploded into a chaos of colors that magically oriented themselves into a viewable picture. It was a miracle, all these shows available with the flick of a switch. In the evenings after dinner I would bask in the flickering blue light of the TV, my elbows on the floor, my legs sprawled out behind me. I was not a particularly discerning viewer, but I watched with childlike concentration whatever happened to be on at the time: "Gilligan's Island," "The Brady Bunch," "The Flintstones," "Wild Wild West."

Now the very mention of these programs evokes a wave of wistful (if slightly embarrassed) nostalgia.

Though the TV was a great way to fill my time, the hours spent in front of it always left me somewhat empty. What was missing, I think, was a sense of wonder. I was to find that this need would best be met by books.

I came late to a love for books.

My earliest books were an assortment of Little Golden Books—those slim, generously illustrated books with a limited page count, an inexpensive price, and a golden spine. If you saw them lined up on a shelf, you could not tell one from another. (In fact, when you *read* them, you often could not tell one from another.) When my own children reached the age where they could enjoy books as more than something to chew on, I was delighted to introduce them to some of the treasures of my own childhood, like *The Pokey Little Puppy.* Many of its remembered charms were lost on me as an adult, however. Perhaps I only treasured it so much because it was one of the few books to escape my little sister's crayon. My books were often the canvas for her earliest artistic endeavors.

I did not come from a family of readers. We had few books in our home growing up, mostly women's magazines and tattered copies of *Reader's Digest*. What books we had were tucked away in a hall closet. Yet I can remember the wonder of certain children's books that I heard read aloud, like A. A. Milne's *Winnie the Pooh*, the Laura Ingalls Wilder books, and *The Phantom Tollbooth*. When I was able to read them for myself, patiently sounding out each word, it was even better.

But the first book that really captured me was a collection of Sherlock Holmes stories. The old black-and-white films starring Basil Rathbone, Nigel Bruce, and a swirling London fog had captured my imagination, and so I looked to a book of Arthur Conan Doyle stories to tell me more about the exploits of Holmes. I quickly became enraptured with these tales, shocked to discover that they were "better than the movies." The difficulty of the language and the unfamiliar British terms were a bit of a challenge, but I understood enough to feel myself swept away. I marveled at Holmes' deductive skills, wanting to be him as he said to an uncomprehending Watson, "The game is afoot." I longed to participate in the pursuit of some brilliant criminal through the dark and winding fog-filled streets of London.

Movies, television, and comic books were still generally preferable to books, though. In my mind, books were always associated with schoolwork. Most of what I read as a young person was to fulfill the requirements of my education, not out of love for the printed page.

I came late to a love for books.

But when it came, it came with a passion.

It began with the desire to search for answers to questions which were beginning to dawn in my high school-aged mind. I was hungry to know more about life and to make sense out of some of my deepest convictions, and books held the promise of being a place I could go to find knowledge and wisdom. I began to read in earnest. What I found would sometimes give me hope and confidence. Other times it would challenge me. And very often it would trouble and unsettle me.

But above all, it would cause me to grow and to change. Whether it was a piece of historical reporting, a story of unfamiliar people and places, or a philosophical meditation, I found myself awakened to new realities. Books, I learned, had purposes other than mere diversion, and I wanted to read as much as my mind and heart could digest, until my eyes grew tired from the strain.

So I began a lifelong adventure, one that has continued to grow in importance to me. Certain books I have read are like road markers, monuments to where I have traveled in my heart and my head in the journey of living.

Books by Homer and Plato and Dante and Shakespeare and Austen and Tolstoy and Dostoevski, which all revealed something of the passion and pathos of what it means to be human.

Books by the poets, which brought to me the beauty of

words and showed me that words themselves could create epiphanies: T.S. Eliot, Donne, Hopkins, Christina Rossetti, Traherne, Wordsworth, and others.

Books by C.S. Lewis, Thomas Merton, Kierkegaard, Pascal, and other writers, which challenged my comfortable middle-class religiosity and made me think about how faith could play a meaningful part in my life.

Books by Dickens and Victor Hugo and Toni Morrison, which reminded me that the world can be a place of great pain, and that compassion and understanding are a necessity for those who want to live humanly.

Books by Mark Helprin, which made me laugh and cry and wonder at the mystery of life, along with novels by the likes of Walker Percy, Frederick Buechner, Graham Greene, Saul Bellow, and David James Duncan.

No matter what his rank or position may be, the lover of books is the richest and the happiest of the children of men.

JOHN ALFRED LANGFORD

As I have grown older, books have only come to play a bigger role in my life. They have helped me to better understand my world and provided hours of entertainment and diversion. They have brightened many an overcast day and brought a sense of realism to moments of self-deception. Because of all that books have done for me, I cannot help but try to point others toward their manifold joys.

I am like the young lover who cannot keep quiet, wanting to extol the wonders of his beloved to anyone who will listen. Friends, and even strangers, are usually willing to hear him out, even if it is with a bemused smile.

I hope you will extend to me that same kind of forbearance.

There is no Frigate like a Book
To take us Lands away
Nor any Coursers like a Page
Of prancing Poetry—
This Traverse may the poorest take
Without oppress of Toll—
How Frugal is the Chariot
That bears the Human Soul.

EMILY DICKINSON

Of all the diversions of life, there is none so proper to fill up its empty spaces as the reading of useful and entertaining authors.

JOSEPH ADDISON

I have sought for happiness everywhere, but I have found it nowhere except in a little corner with a little book.

THOMAS À KEMPIS

One of the most wonderful modern celebrations of books and reading can be found in Helene Hanff's *84 Charing Cross Road*, a collection of letters between a London bookseller and an American bibliophile. Here is a sample letter, written upon receiving a lovely used copy of one of John Henry Newman's books.

October 15, 1950

WELL!!!

All I have to say to YOU, Frank Doel, is we live in depraved, destructive and degenerate times when a bookshop—a BOOKSHOP—starts tearing up beautiful old books to use as wrapping paper. I said to John Henry when he stepped out of it:

"Would you believe a thing like that, Your Eminence?" and he said he wouldn't. You tore that book up in the middle of a major battle and I don't even know which war it was.

The Newman arrived almost a week ago and I'm just beginning to recover. I keep it on the table with me all day, every now and then I stop typing and reach over and touch it. Not because it's a first edition; I just never saw a book so beautiful. I feel vaguely guilty about owning it. All that gleaming leather and gold stamping and beautiful type belongs in the pine-panelled library of an English country home; it wants to be read by the fire in a gentleman's leather easy chair—not on a secondhand studio couch in a one-room hovel in a broken-down brownstone front.

I want the Q [Arthur Quiller-Couch] anthology. I'm not sure how much it was, I lost your last letter. I think it was about two bucks, I'll enclose two singles; if I owe you more let me know.

Why don't you wrap it in pages LCXII and LCXIII so I can at least find out who won the battle and what war it was?

HH

P.S. Have you got Sam Pepys' diary over there? I need him for long winter evenings.

There is a great deal of difference between the eager man who wants to read a book, and the tired man who wants a book to read. A man reading a Le Queux mystery wants to get to the end of it. A man reading the Dickens novel wished that it might never end.

GEORGE MACDONALD

Book love, my friend, is your pass to the greatest, the purest, and the most perfect pleasure that God has prepared for His creatures. It lasts when all other pleasures fade. It will support you when all other recreations are gone. It will last until your death. It will make your hours pleasant to you as long as you live.

ANTHONY TROLLOPE

A classic is a book that has never finished saying what it has to say.

ITALO CALVINO

What a joy there is in a good book, writ by some great master of thought, who breaks into beauty as in summer the meadow into grass and dandelions and violets with geraniums and manifold sweetness.

THEODORE PARKER

If the crowns of all the kingdoms of
Europe were laid down at my feet
in exchange for my books and
my love of reading, I
would spurn them all.

FRANCOIS FÉNELON

It is from books that wise men derive
consolation in the troubles of life.

VICTOR HUGO

We settle to read any work of fiction
with the same squirm of anticipation primitive people
experienced as they gathered closer to the fire
and the storyteller began the tale.

JENNY DE VRIES

Katherine Mansfield, herself an accomplished writer, was a greater lover of books.

...During the past two nights I have read The Dynasts. *Isn't it queer how a book eludes one. And then suddenly it opens for you? I have looked into this book before now. But the night before last when I opened it I suddenly understood what the poet meant, and how he meant it should be read! The point of view which is like a light streaming from the imagination and over the imagination—over one's head as it were—the chorus and the aerial music.*

Letter to John Middleton Murray
May 24, 1921

In fact, isn't it a joy—there is hardly a greater one—to find a new book, a living book, and to know that it will remain with you while life lasts?...

Letter to John Middleton Murray
February 7, 1922

If there is a book to be read, no matter how bad that book is, I read it. I will read it. Was it always so with me?

Journal entry, 1922

Sitting last winter among my books, and walled round with all the comfort and protection which they and my fireside could afford me,—to wit, a table of high-piled books at my back, my writing desk to one side of me, some shelves on the other, and the feeling of the warm fire at my feet,—I began to consider how I loved the authors of those books; how I loved them too, not only for the imaginative pleasures they afforded me, but for their making me love the very books themselves, and delight to be in contact with them. I looked sideways at my Spencer, my Theocritus, and my *Arabian Nights;* then above them at my Italian Poets; then behind me at my Dryden and Pope, my Romances, and my Boccaccio; then on my left side at my Chaucer, who lay on my writing desk; and thought how natural it was in Charles Lamb to give a kiss to an old folio, as I once saw him do to Chapman's Homer....At all events, nothing, while I live and think, can deprive me of my value for such treasures. I can help the appreciation of them while I last, and love them till I die; and perhaps, if fortune turns her face once more in kindness upon me before I go, I may chance, some quiet day, to lay my over-beating temples on a book, and so have the death I most envy.

LEIGH HUNT
My Books

"Girls," said Meg seriously, looking from the tumbled head beside her to the two little night-capped ones in the room beyond, "mother wants us to read and love and mind these books, and we must begin at once. We used to be faithful about it; but since father went away, and all this war trouble unsettled us, we have neglected many things. You can do as you please; but I shall keep my book on the table here, and read a little every morning as soon as I wake, for I know it will do me good, and help me through the day."

Then she opened her new book and began to read. Jo put her arm round her, and, leaning cheek to cheek, read also, with the quiet expression so seldom seen on her restless face.

LOUISA MAY ALCOTT
Little Women

When you reread a classic you do not see more in the book than you did before; you see more in you than was there before.

CLIFTON FADIMAN

They are for company the best friends, in doubts counselors, in damps comforters, time's perspective, the home-traveler's ship or horse, the busy man's best recreation, the opiate of idle weariness, the mind's best ordinary, nature's garden, and the seed-plot of immortality.

BULSTRODE WHITELOCKE

O, let my books be
then the eloquence
And dumb presagers of
my speaking breast;
Who plead for love
and for recompense
More than that tongue
that hath more express'd.

WILLIAM SHAKESPEARE

CHAPTER 2

A PLACE TO READ

Sometimes our memories of certain books are intimately connected with the places we first read them. I remember reading Anne Tyler's *Saint Maybe*, a melancholy tale about devotion to and love of family, during a series of plane flights on a long business trip. I was lonely, pensive, and far away from home. As I read, I frequently found myself blinking back tears and trying to hide my deep emotional (and somewhat unexpected) response. People sitting around me averted their eyes and shifted in their seats. But there in the plane, lifted up above the clouds, I also felt lifted out of the patterns of my own life. I was able to survey my priorities and goals with a new clarity. The book softened me and made me feel strangely vulnerable, providing the impetus for some important soul-searching and self-examination, as I stared out the window of the plane.

I remember as well the two weeks I gave to reading Mark Helprin's massive, marvel-filled cornucopia of a book, *A Soldier of the Great War.* During those two weeks, everything in my life seemed suffused with a supernatural radiance, a glow that emanated from this magnificent novel. I recall driving to work one morning, preoccupied with the beauty I had gathered from this book, and noticed for the first time the loveliness of a tree I had passed by so unthinkingly hundreds of times before.

I remember reading most of Thomas à Kempis' astringent devotional classic *On the Imitation of Christ* in the quiet of a big city hotel room where I sat feeling alone and somewhat disconnected from the world. It was the third time I had read it, but somehow this time was different. I didn't have to be anywhere for several hours and there were no demands on my time. The sun slanting through the raindrops on the window and the gentle hiss of traffic on the rain-slick street below seemed to slow me down enough to really take in the message of the book.

A friend told me she will never forget sitting propped up against a tombstone reading *Wuthering Heights* in the crumbling cemetery just down the street from her dormitory room. Somehow that seems appropriate.

Libraries are a good place to read, surrounded by thousands of books while one lays claim to your undivided attention. One friend told me that he had a special corner on the third floor of the Stanford University Library. He could retreat from the stresses of the academic world and spend time reading or maybe just thinking about life. It was quiet there, and the place felt like it belonged to him alone.

Planes, trains, and buses provide opportunities to read while you draw ever nearer to your destination.…I fly regularly and cherish the uninterrupted moments for reading. I have also discovered that the rhythmic clack and rumble of a train on its tracks makes the perfect accompaniment to reading. The words flow by in measured beats, in harmony with the passing scenery and the mottled light playing upon the page.

The outdoors can be a marvelous place to read, accompanied by the quiet drone of buzzing insects. Sometimes it takes an extra bit of effort to keep the wind from prematurely turning your pages, but certain types of books, such as Wordsworth's poetry, are always better in the company of a tree with rustling leaves.

The seashore can also be a good place, where you can pause over a passage, look up and focus for a moment on the distant horizon while your thoughts focus and you ponder what you have read. The medieval monks might have done well to establish their monasteries right on the coastline.

What is the *perfect* environment for reading? Well, obviously it won't be the same for everyone, but here is mine: a quiet room with a wing back chair, surrounded by

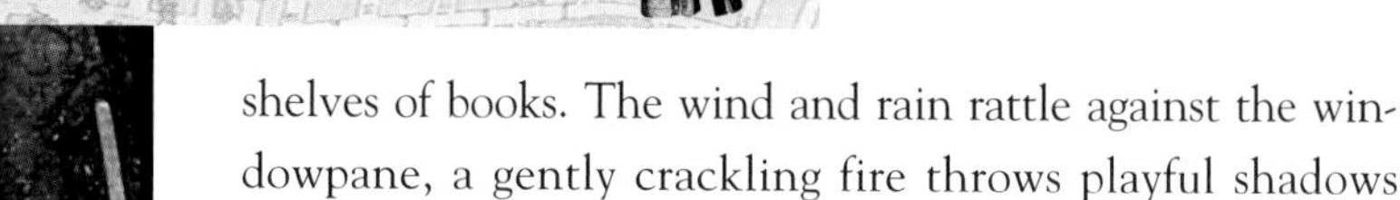

shelves of books. The wind and rain rattle against the windowpane, a gently crackling fire throws playful shadows across the floor. Add a cup of tea near at hand, and you have my ideal of the perfect spot to lose yourself in a book.

When we read we may not only be kings and live in palaces, but, what is far better, we may transport ourselves to the mountains or the seashore, and visit the most beautiful parts of the earth, without fatigue, inconvenience, or expense.

JOHN LUBBOCK

But even when you cannot find the perfect spot, if the book is good enough it will not matter too much. A good book will take you to places you have never been and give you the sights and sounds and smells of a thousand exotic locations. It is a passport that knows no boundaries.

When you lose yourself in a book, that is the place where, for that moment, you truly are.

Find the most comfortable position: seated, stretched out, curled up, or lying flat....Stretch your legs, go ahead and put your feet on a cushion, on two cushions, on the arms of the sofa, on the wings of the chair, on the coffee table, on the desk, on the piano, on the globe. Take your shoes off first....Adjust the light so you won't strain your eyes. Do it now, because once you're absorbed in reading there will be no budging you.

ITALO CALVINO

The familiar faces of my books welcomed me. I threw myself into my reading chair and gazed around me with pleasure. All my old friends present—there in spirit, ready to talk with me any moment when I was in the mood, making no claim upon my attention when I was not.

George MacDonald

An 1878 book on interior decorating speaks of the importance of books as part of the home's furnishing:

For lovers of books... a house without books is no house at all; and in a family where books make a great part of the pleasure of living, they must be where they can be got at without trouble, and what is of more importance, where they can share in the life about them and receive some touches of the humanity they supply and feed.

Clarence Cook
The House Beautiful

The organized soul has one book beside the bed. The glutton sleeps with a New York skyline lurching an inch from the bed.

CHARLOTTE GRAY

If you cannot read all your books, at any rate handle, or as it were, fondle them—peer into them, let them fall open where they will, read from the first sentence that arrests the eye, set them back on the shelves with your own hands, arrange them on your own plan so that you at least know where they are. Let them be your friends; let them at any rate be your acquaintances.

WINSTON CHURCHILL

Books, books, books. It was not that I read so much. I read and re-read the same ones. But all of them were necessary to me. Their presence, their smell, the letters of their titles, and the texture of their leather bindings.

COLETTE

There is a class of street-readers, whom I never contemplate without affection — the poor gentry, who, not having the wherewithal to buy or hire a book, filch a little learning at the open stalls— the owner, with his hard eye, casting envious looks at them all the while, and thinking when they will have done. Venturing tenderly, page after page, expecting every moment he shall interpose his interdict, and yet unable to deny themselves the gratification, they "snatch a fearful joy."

CHARLES LAMB

The Last Essays of Elia

Emily Post shares how essential books are to the proper preparation of a guest room:

There must of course be a night light at the head of the bed. Not just a decorative glow-worm effect, but a 40 watt light with an adjustable shade that is really good to lie in bed and read by. And always there should be books—chosen more to divert than to strain the reader's attention. The sort of selection appropriate for a guest room might best comprise two or three books of the moment, a light novel, or a mystery novel, a book of essays or poetry, another of short stories, and a few of the best magazines. Better yet, books ought to be chosen particularly, for even though one may not guess accurately the tastes of another, one can at least guess whether the visitor is likely to prefer transcendental philosophy or detective stories, and provide accordingly.

EMILY POST

Often have I sighed to measure
By myself a lonely pleasure,
Sighed to think I read a book
Only read, perhaps, by me.

WILLIAM WORDSWORTH

While living in New York, I acquired the habit of rarely going out without tucking a book or magazine under my arm. Vibrant and fascinating though New York can be, it has so many parts and patches that are best read through: riding subways, standing in bank lines, arranging any sort of bureaucratic business, sitting through traffic jams. New York probably offers more good reasons to avert one's eyes than any other city in America, and where better to avert them than into a book? To this day, though long removed from New York, I still usually walk about with a book in hand, and I keep a book or two in my car, often getting in a quick paragraph at a stoplight. If you happen to be behind me, please don't honk when the light turns green, for I could be coming to the end of a paragraph.

JOSEPH EPSTEIN

The end of reading is not more books but more life.

HOLBROOK JACKSON

Just the knowledge that a good book is waiting one at the end of a long day makes that day happier.

KATHLEEN NORRIS

A small breakfast-room adjoined the drawing-room, I slipped in there. It contained a bookcase: I soon possessed myself of a volume, taking care that it should be one stored with pictures. I mounted into the window-seat: gathering up my feet, I sat cross-legged, like a Turk; and, having drawn the red moreen curtain nearly closed, I was shrined in double retirement.

Folds of scarlet drapery shut in my view to the right hand; to the left were the clear panes of glass, protecting, but not separating me from the drear November day. At intervals,

while turning over the leaves of my book, I studied the aspect of that winter afternoon. Afar, it offered a pale blank of mist and cloud; near a scene of wet lawn and storm-beat shrub, with ceaseless rain sweeping away wildly before a long and lamentable blast.

CHARLOTTE BRONTE
Jane Eyre

Only one hour in the normal day is more pleasurable than the hour spent in bed with a book before going to sleep, and that is the hour spent in bed with a book after being called in the morning.

ROSE MACAULEY

CHAPTER 3

OUR CHILDHOOD COMPANIONS

Do you remember when you first learned to read? Can you recall the wonder of the time when you began to unlock the mystery behind the ordered black characters that stretched across the white spaces of an open book? It was a feeling of mastery, of entering into a larger world, of emerging from the confines of your own life into the wider world beyond.

When I talk with people about their experiences of reading as a child, the word that never fails to come up is "magical." The book was a vehicle that helped them travel to places they'd never been, never heard of, or never even imagined. Discovering the joy in these books launched a lifetime of adventure.

Do you remember? Curled up in your bed at night or stretched out on the floor in a patch of sunlight, the stories took you out of yourself. They helped you imagine new selves. Through the magic of imagination you were present with the heroes and heroines of the books you read. You felt the rush of adrenaline, the shortness of breath, the swelling in the heart, the anger, the pain, the hope, and the dreams of the characters. And like most children, you visited these stories again and again. They created memories for you that were as authentic as anything you'd actually experienced in the "real world."

Can you remember special moments from the books of your childhood?

> ***My education was the liberty I had to read indiscriminately and all the time, with my eyes hanging out.***
>
> DYLAN THOMAS

...Winnie the Pooh and Piglet's fumbling attempts to make something special of Eeyore's nearly forgotten birthday and his simple joy in the broken balloon and the empty honey pot.

...Alice's attempts to make sense out of her encounters with the Chesire Cat, the Mad Hatter, and the wicked Queen of Hearts as she learns something about the delightful absurdities of life.

...Toad and Ratty's transcendent moment of breathless wonder as they glimpse the Piper at the Gates of Dawn.

...The gentle kinship and respect that grows between Huck Finn and Jim as they make their way down the Mississippi.

...The joyous strains of Pa Ingalls' fiddle, even in the dead of winter and during the most precarious of times for Laura and her family.

...The Cowardly Lion, the Tin Man and the Scarecrow, all coming to realize that what they really need lies within their grasp, and Dorothy's realization that the power to return home was always right under her nose.

...Aslan's resurrection, which brings an end to the everlasting winter as he breathes new life into the land and into the hearts of Lucy, Edmund, Peter, and Susan.

These are memories as real as anything we might have experienced. They touched us, challenged us, and caused us to see ourselves and our world in new ways. The characters from the books of our early years allowed us to dream along with them and make the most of the fragility of childhood.

And then, one day, the experience of reading changes forever. The dreams of childhood are replaced by the harsh realities of an adult world where magic and mystery are in short supply. Consider Christopher Robin and Pooh standing in the enchanted place at the edge of the hundred acre wood as Christopher Robin explains (as best as he can understand it) the new phase of his life that he is entering. "I'm not going to do Nothing any more," he says wistfully.

"Never again?" queries Pooh.

"Well, not so much. They don't let you."

But do we have to lose that sense of innocence and enchantment we found in books as children? I don't think so. When I recently read *The Phantom Tollbooth* to my two daughters, I took no less delight in it than I had as a child. I laughed at its clever humor and was caught up in the surprising twists of its storyline. It graciously provided something I still need in my life: enchantment. Perhaps one of the things our world needs most is to be "reenchanted," to remember the glory of the simple things we treasured as children. Perhaps we need to rediscover the gift of doing Nothing, of letting our dreams take us where they will. Perhaps we need to set aside our seriousness and rediscover the books that captured our hearts as children.

They are still there waiting for us.

No book is really worth reading at the age of ten which is not equally (and often far more) worth reading at the age of fifty and beyond.

C. S. LEWIS

If my life had been more full of calamity than it has been, I would live it over again to have read the books I did in my youth.

WILLIAM HAZLITT

It is the books we read before middle life that do most to mold our characters and influence our lives.

ROBERT PITMAN

The books that charmed us in youth recall the delight ever afterwards; we are hardly persuaded there are any like them, any deserving equally of our affections. Fortunate if the best fall in our way during this susceptible and forming period of our lives.

A. BRONSON ALCOTT

When I was a child I loved to read. I loved Jane Eyre *especially and read it over and over. I didn't know anyone else who liked to read except my mother, and it got me in a lot of trouble because it made me into a thief and a liar. I stole books, and I stole money to buy them....Books brought me the greatest satisfaction. Just to be alone, reading, under the house, with lizards and spiders running around...*

JAMAICA KINCAID

For children, the joy of a book is not merely the story but the feel, the taste, the smell of it — the texture of the paper, the size and shape of the typeface, the illustrations, flaws, marks, even the numbering of the pages. My Peter Pan *was the cheapest of editions, with an indented* Mabel Lucy Atwell Peter *on the red cover. The paper was thick, the illustration line drawings set into the text. I still know that little book as if I held it in my hands. The memory holds the cold air of my bedroom, the night light in its saucer, the car lights crossing the ceiling, my father's voice.*

PAMELA BROWN

There is a space on everyone's bookshelves for books one has outgrown but cannot give away. They hold one's youth between their leaves, like flowers pressed on a half-forgotten summer's day.

MARION C. GARRETTY

My father had left a small collection of books in a little room upstairs, to which I had access (for it adjoined my own) and which nobody else in our house ever troubled. From that blessed little room, Roderick Random, Peregrine Pickle, Humphrey Clinker, Tom Jones, the Vicar of Wakefield, Don Quixote, Gil Blas, and Robinson Crusoe came out, a glorious host, to keep me company. They kept alive my fancy, and my hope of something beyond that place and time,—they, and the Arabian Nights, *and the* Tales of the Genii,*—and did me no harm; for whatever harm was in some of them was not there for me; I knew nothing of it. It is astonishing to me now, how I found time, in the midst of my porings and blunderings over heavier themes, to read those books as I did.*

This was my only and my constant comfort. When I think of it, the picture always rises in my mind, of a summer evening, the boys at play in the churchyard, and I sitting on my bed, reading as if for life.

CHARLES DICKENS
David Copperfield

I learned from the age of two or three that any room in our house, at any time of day, was there to read in, or to be read to. My mother read to me. She'd read to me in the big bedroom in the mornings, when we were in her rocker together, which ticked in rhythm as we rocked, as though we had a cricket accompanying the story. She'd read to me in the dining room on winter afternoons in front of the coal fire, with our cuckoo clock ending the story with "Cuckoo," and at night when I'd got in my own bed. I must have given her no peace. Sometimes she read to me in the kitchen while she sat churning, and the churning sobbed along with any story. It was my ambition to have her read to me while I churned; once she granted my wish, but she read off my story before I brought her butter. She was an expressive reader. When she was reading "Puss in Boots," for instance, it was impossible not to know that she distrusted all cats.

It had been startling and disappointing to me to find out that storybooks had been written by people, that books were not natural wonders, coming up of themselves like grass. Yet regardless of where they came from, I cannot remember a time when I was not in love with them—with the books themselves, cover and binding and the paper they were printed on, with their smell and their weight and with their possession in my arms, captured and carried off to myself. Still illiterate, I was ready for them, committed to all the reading I could give them.

EUDORA WELTY

One Writer's Beginnings

What I sought in books was imagination. It was depth, depth of thought and feeling; some sort of extreme of subject matter; some nearness to death; some call to courage. I myself was getting wild; I wanted wildness, originality, genius, rapture, hope. I wanted strength, not tea parties. What I sought in books was a world whose surfaces, whose people and events and days lived, actually matched the exaltation of the interior life. There you could live.

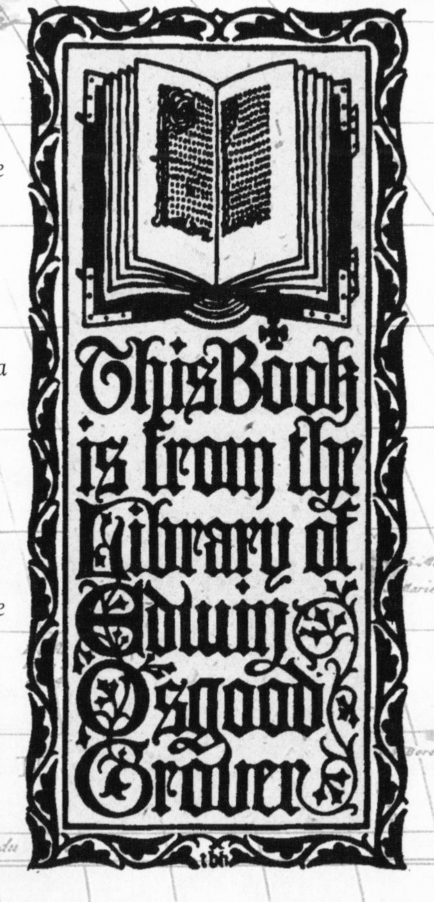

Those of us who read carried a secret around with us like martyrs a secret knowledge, a secret joy, and a secret hope: There is a life worth living where history is still taking place; there are ideas worth dying for, and circumstances where courage is still prized. This life could be found and joined, like the Resistance. I kept this exhilarating faith alive in myself, concealed under my uniform shirt like an oblate's ribbon; I would not be parted from it.

ANNIE DILLARD
An American Childhood

I am a product of long corridors, empty sunlit rooms, upstairs indoor silences, attics explored in solitude, distant noises of gurgling cisterns and pipes, and the noise of wind under the tiles. Also, of endless books. My father bought all the books he read and never got rid of any of them. There were books in the study, books in the drawing room, books in the cloakroom, books (two deep) in the great bookcase on the landing, books in a bedroom, books piled as high as my shoulder in the cistern attic, books of all kinds reflecting every transient stage of my parents' interest, books readable and unreadable, books suitable for a child and books most emphatically not. Nothing was forbidden me. In the seemingly endless rainy afternoons I took volume after volume from the shelves. I had always the same certainty of finding a book that was new to me as a man who walks into a field has of finding a new blade of grass.

C. S. Lewis
Surprised by Joy

My early and invincible love of reading,...I would not exchange for the treasures of India.
EDWARD GIBBON

Anne was curled up Turk-fashion on the hearthrug, gazing into that joyous glow where the sunshine of a hundred summers was being distilled form the maple cordwood. She had been reading, but her book had slipped to the floor, and now she was dreaming, with a smile on her parted lips. Glittering castles in Spain were shaping themselves out of the mists and rainbows of her lively fancy; adventures wonderful and enthralling were happening to her in cloudland—adventures that always turned out triumphantly and never involved her in scrapes like those of actual life.
LUCY MAUD MONTGOMERY
Anne of Green Gables

CHAPTER 4

NO PLACE LIKE A BOOKSTORE

A good bookstore is one of the most comforting places on earth. On the shelves surrounding you, a written record of the human experience awaits. Books on war fight for shelf space with books on peace, books on romantic love nestle close to books on jealousy and murder, faith and doubt sit next to one another along with books of history and books of fantasy. All that is human or part of the created world is celebrated, questioned, analyzed, or revealed in all its splendor. What Chaucer wrote in another context applies to the bookstore: "Here is all God's plenty." If somehow a person could read all, or even a great deal, of what is offered in a bookstore, he would be so unfathomably rich in vicarious experiences, ageless wisdom, and the facts which summarize our knowledge. Of course, time does not allow us that privilege.

That is why a bookstore is a place of choices.

In a bookstore we feel free and sovereign. We make our own choices from the rich backlog of old books or the thousands of new titles published every year. And so we browse, grazing over the luxuriant meadow of choices that stretches out before us. In the process, we will pick up any number of potential reads and weigh them in our hands. We will skim them, perhaps studying the table of contents, or maybe just opening them up at random and reading the first little bit that our eyes settle on. As the guest at a sumptuous banquet, we will sample any number of dishes before we finally settle on those one or two that will become our literary feast.

What is it that attracts you to a book? Is it the title, playfully clever or redolent with cherished associations? Or the cover, designed to catch our eye by

its outrageousness or lure us in by its beauty? Or do you seek knowledge of a particular subject or wish to introduce yourself to an unknown realm of knowledge? Or could it be that you recognize the author, by her distinguished reputation or because you have formerly fallen under the spell of his gift for spinning words together? Whatever it is, when we are stricken, after all our searching, with the conviction that we simply must have *that* particular book, we dig into our wallets knowing that this will be money well spent.

> ***When I get a little money, I buy books; and if there is any left I buy food and clothes.***
>
> DESIDERIUS ERASMUS

The modern bookstore, with its careful organization, adequate lighting, and balanced stock of titles, can be a wonderful place to while away a rainy autumn afternoon. Although we may frequent any number of bookstores in our area, most of us have a favorite haunt, a bookstore which just feels more comfortable and inviting than the others. We go here to partake of the strange communal solitude that book lovers share. A favorite bookstore is a place whose layout we know well, a place where we know the contents of the shelves so intimately that it is easy to spot a new addition. And on any given trip we may be rewarded by discovering a fascinating, just-released volume on a subject of abiding interest, or, most gratifying of all, a brand new title from a favorite author, one of our literary soul-mates.

But if we are looking for unknown literary gems, one of the best places to find them is in a used bookstore. The used bookstore contains a wholly different set of charms. Oftentimes, the organization is not apparent to anyone other than the dusty old man in the fraying sweater who keeps watch over his preserve of antiquarian treasures. No matter how we rack our brains, we cannot make any sense of his system. All the better for us, for this opens up the possibility of discovery. Instead of looking for what we know we want, we are forced to slow down and peruse the stacks for hidden treasures. Who knows what jewel might lie on the next shelf down, tucked in there between that volume on Scottish history and the book of Caravaggio prints. In a used bookstore, we are archaeologists. We never know what fine literary artifact we might uncover next.

Of course, the search is made more challenging by the shelves which strain to contain their load, the books piled whilly-nilly on top of books, the stacks which fill every unused corner and creep into the aisles, as well as the ever-present random boxes of unshelved titles, which are both a potential navigational hazard in the cramped quarters and sometimes the best place to look for that hard-to-find volume.

The used book store is a home for orphans, for those books rejected by their original owner. When we adopt them into our own family of reading materials, we promise, as it were, to provide them with a place to call home. Sometimes we stand in a used bookstore with a volume in our hand and marvel over the foolishness of someone who would rid themselves of such a glorious treasure. "How could they?" we mutter to ourselves as we smile at our own wisdom.

And yet, how many times have I regretted the loss of a book that I once offered to the used book buyer?

Such is the great cycle of book buying. Every book was once new, and probably once treasured, if only for a short time. When we are done with it and cast it aside, it will likely find itself someday on the shelves of another reader. Unlike many things, a book is never totally without value. There is always someone out there who would treasure it.

One of the most distinguished personages in Europe, showing his library to a visitor, observed that not only this collection, but all his social successes in life, he traced back to "the first franc he saved from the cake shop to spend at a bookstall."

UNKNOWN

When you sell a man a book you don't sell him just twelve ounces of paper and ink and glue—you sell him a whole new life. Love and friendship and humor and ships at sea by night—there's all heaven and earth in a book, a real book I mean.

CHRISTOPHER MORLEY

That I can read and be happy while I am reading, is a great blessing. Could I have remembered, as some men do, what I read, I should have been able to call myself an educated man. But that power I have never possessed. Something is always left—something dim and inaccurate—but still something sufficient to preserve the taste for more. I am inclined to think that it is so with most readers.

ANTHONY TROLLOPE
Autobiography

Harold Laski writes to former chief justice Oliver Wendell Holmes, Jr. about an experience in book-buying:

I had an amusing book-adventure. I found a nice copy of a 16th-century Aristotle—the Politics*—with a coat of arms on the binding. I paid ten shillings for it and then went on to a shop where the bookseller payed me to re-sell it to him. I changed it there for a nice Locke in four quarto volumes. When these came home, Alexander, the philosopher, was having tea here. I opened the Locke and he immediately sighed with envy and offered to exchange something for them. I acquiesced and am now the possessor of John Adam's* Works *in ten volumes. Frida [his wife] is urgent that the process of exchange should stop there lest I end up with the Law Reports and drive her to found a new house.*

HAROLD J. LASKI

Where is the human nature so weak as in the bookstore?
HENRY WARD BEECHER
If a book is worth reading, it is worth buying.
JOHN RUSKIN

For books are not absolutely dead things, but do contain a potency of life in them to be as active as that soul was whose progeny they are; nay, they do preserve as in a vial the purest

efficacy and extraction of that living intellect that bred them. I know they are as lively, and are as vigorously productive, as those fabulous dragon's teeth; and being sown up and down, may chance to spring up armed men. And yet, on the other hand, unless wariness be used, as good almost kill a man as kill a good book. Who kills a man kills a reasonable creature, God's image; but he who destroys a good book, kills reason itself, kills the image of God, as it were in the eye. Many a man lives a burden to the earth; but a good book is the precious life-blood of a master spirit, embalmed and treasured up on purpose to a life beyond life. 'Tis true, no age of life can restore a life, whereof perhaps there is not great loss; and revolutions of ages do not oft recover the loss of a rejected truth, for the want of which whole nations fare the worse.

JOHN MILTON
Areopagitica

In the Jewish tradition books were honored as physical objects because of what they represented. Here Jiri Langer writes of how greatly a book was esteemed among the Hasidic community:

Books are greatly respected here, worshipped, in fact. Nobody, for instance, sits on a bench if there is a book anywhere on it. That would be an affront to the book. We never leave a book face downwards or upside down, but always face upwards. If a book falls to the ground we pick it up and kiss it. When we have finished reading we kiss the book before we put it away. To throw it aside, or put other things on top of it is a sin. Yet the books are nearly all woefully dilapidated by constant use. When a book is so badly torn that it cannot be used, the caretaker takes it to the cemetery and buries it.

We never leave books open except when we are actually learning from them. If we are obliged to slip away for a moment, and do not wish to close the book, we may leave it open so as not to lose the place, but we must cover it with a cloth. If anyone notices another person going away from a book without closing or covering it, he goes over and shuts it himself; but first he will look at the open page and read a few lines of it. If he were to shut the book without reading it at all, his act of closing it would weaken the power of memorizing in the other person who left the book open. The parchment scroll of the Law, which is hand-written, is held in even greater respect than printed books.

JIRI LANGER

Nine Gates to the Chassidic Mysteries

CHAPTER 5

THE LURE OF LIBRARIES

Libraries are magical places. They are places of wonder, places outside the hustle and bustle of our all too busy lives where we can lose ourselves in a book-created reverie. The books are arrayed on the shelves like inviting portals into other worlds. We crack open the covers and our eyes settle upon the words. The letters dance before our eyes momentarily, like an unknown language, but in short order they lose their foreign aspect. Then the words themselves disappear, forgotten. We are caught up and carried by the images they evoke. They are ladders by which we climb out of ourselves.

The charms of the library are many, one of them being its smell—the smell of stored knowledge mingled with library paste. A new book and an old book each have their own fragrance. The older volumes carry the faint scent of decay, of books returning to the elements out of which they were formed. The new books, on the other hand, exude a crisp freshness, a slightly sweet aroma combining newly imprinted ink and the glue that holds the spine together. Both can be found in abundance in the library.

Another charm is that each library book has its own history. The old style pocket and due date slip gave us an idea of how frequently a book had been read and sometimes even told us by whom. We could gauge a book's popularity by how often it had been borrowed. For the true bibliophile there is a unique pleasure in pulling a book from the shelf and finding that you are the first to lay claim to it in many years. And though I understand the necessity of the new computerized check-out systems, I am somewhat mournful of the historical loss this entails.

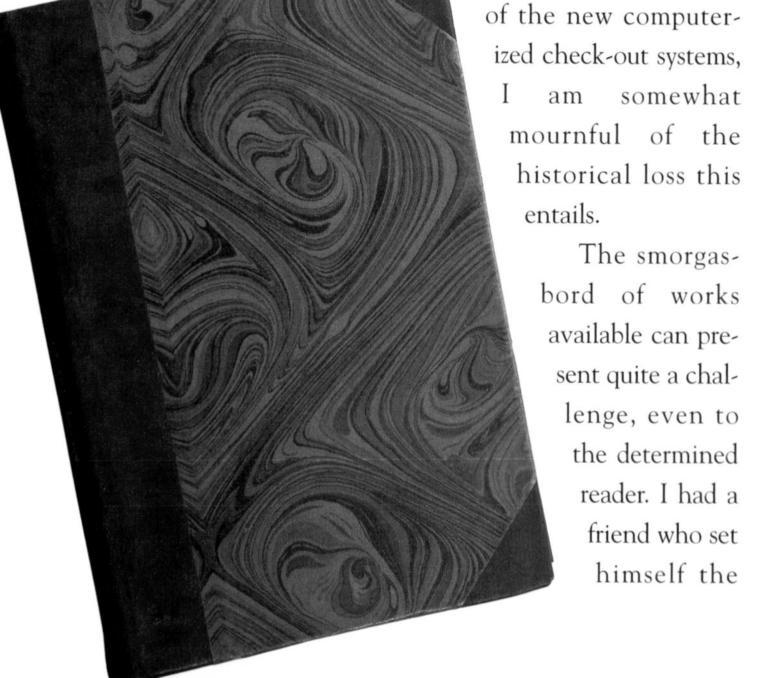

The smorgasbord of works available can present quite a challenge, even to the determined reader. I had a friend who set himself the goal of systematically reading through every book in the school library, beginning with the first digits of the Dewey Decimal System. Predictably, he made it no further than a third of the way through the first shelf, abandoning the project after the fifth straight book on the same obscure topic.

Such a project did not surprise me. Deep inside I long to know, to order the vast panorama of human knowledge, to organize my thoughts, to possess understanding. The library holds the promise of having gathered together in one place all the disparate facts and accumulated knowledge that make up the summation of human experience. Unlike the bookstore, here it is all free for the taking (or at least for the borrowing). Every week you can return to gather an armful of potential pleasure at only the cost of a signature on a library card. Some of the best things in life really are free!

> ***Never lend books, for no one ever returns them; the only books I have in my library are books that other folks have lent me.***
>
> ANATOLE FRANCE

Unless of course, we do not return our books on time. Then the charges begin to mount—along with the embarrassment. One of my dear friends claims that she and her sister paid so many overdue fines over the years that they single-handedly financed the building of a new wing in the local library. And not every book gets returned, no matter how good our intentions. Probably few personal libraries are completely free of volumes that somehow never got returned, books whose overdue fees have continued to mount since 1971.

Libraries are silent places in a noisy world, places where a person can reflect upon their life, distracted only by the gentle rustling of pages, the jostling of books being taken from and returned to their shelves, and an occasional cough.

It is a place of order in a world that is eminently disordered. In the library there is a resting place for every fact, a home for every subject. Even if our own minds are cluttered and chaotic, we can always depend on the card catalog to help us find what we need.

Sometimes the tidiness and organization of the library can reach such an extreme that a librarian actually comes to resent the intrusion of a reader into their ordered little world. I remember a school librarian whose face always tightened when you brought a book to the counter to check out. There was a look in her eyes as if to say: If you *really* must leave the building with that book, you'd better take good care of it and get it back on time. I wonder if she sometimes wept tears late at night over the prodigal books that had never been returned?

A public library, however, is no replacement for a personal library. The true lover of books wants to be surrounded by them. Over the years the books accumulate. And once acquired, they are always hard to part with. A good book becomes a friend, however neglected it might sometimes be. Even when you scratch your head and cannot remember why you ever purchased a particular volume, it is not always easy to give it up. Through the passing of years it has claimed its rightful place as a resident of your shelves.

My personal library is a reflection of who I am, a record

of the meanderings of my mind, attesting to transient interests and curiosities pursued. I often refer to my own library, large and ever expanding, as my "adjacent brain." It is a storehouse for ideas and information, all of which I could never manage to stuff into my cranial cavity. Countless wonders, intriguing ideas, infuriating arguments, paradoxical puzzles, soul-stirring stories, empirical facts, and spiritual resources—all this is as close as my bookshelves.

Even when I do not open their covers, just the very sight of my books gives me a sense of peace as I meditate on the history of my relationship with each volume. I can remember when I first acquired a certain book, my first reading of it, and the various times I have had need to look into it. And still it is there waiting for me should I ever have need to refer to it again.

Wherever books are gathered together, whether in an elaborate library of vast dimension or on a couple of shelves constructed of boards and concrete blocks, we find the amazing productivity of the human mind and imagination. And we can rejoice that we are able to have such ready access to it.

A home without books is like a room without windows...A little library, growing every year, is an honorable part of a man's history. It is a man's duty to have books. A library is not a luxury, but one of the necessities of life.

HENRY WARD BEECHER

Miss Bingley's attention was quite as much engaged in watching Mr. Darcy's progress through his book, as in reading her own; and she was perpetually either making some inquiry, or looking at his page. She could not win him, however, to any conversation; he merely answered her question, and read on. At length, quite exhausted by the attempt to be amused with her own book, which she had only chosen because it was the second volume of his, she gave a great yawn and said, "How pleasant it is to spend an evening in this way! I declare after all there is no enjoyment like reading! How much sooner one tires of anything than of a book! When I have a house of my own, I shall be miserable if I have not an excellent library."

JANE AUSTEN
Pride and Prejudice

Nothing can supply the place of books. They are cheering or soothing companions in solitude, illness, affliction. The wealth of both continents would not compensate for the good they impart. Let every man, if possible, gather some good books under his roof, and obtain access for himself and family to some social library. Almost any luxury should be sacrificed to this.

W. E. CHANNING

When we are collecting books, we are collecting happiness.

VINCENT STARRETT

Books are a delightful society. If you go into a room filled with books, even without taking them down from their shelves, they seem to speak to you, to welcome you.

WILLIAM E. GLADSTONE

Under the great dome of the British Museum's reading room (second in size only to St. Peter's) I sat reading a modern English novel, while all around me scholars from the world over rustled the pages of heavier works, coughed dryly, cracked their knuckles, and took notes. My friend from Johns Hopkins thumbed through volume after volume of Latin works, preparing a book about atheism in Renaissance literature. Surely this was an incongruous place for one to read a modern work of fiction. And yet nowhere else could I find a copy of The Pied Piper of Lovers, *the one book lacking in my Lawrence Durrell collection.*

In an hour of reading I had reaped the information I sought, and was startled by the novel's penultimate scene: the same great circular reading room in which I sat. I closed the book and went to claim the seventeenth-century volumes paged and awaiting me in the north reading room, made arrangements for photostats of certain pages, then went out to lunch.

Many years had passed since I had last read in the British Museum, and I returned bearing the usual letter of credential for admittance. It was not needed; my original card, dated 1931, was in its proper place in the active file, and had only to be renewed. This sort of continuity is taken for granted in Britain, yet I never ceased to be impressed by it, coming as I did from California, where roots are shallow.

LAWRENCE CLARK POWELL
Books in My Baggage

"I am astonished," said Miss Bingley, "that my father should have left so small a collection of books. What a delightful library you have at Pemberley, Mr. Darcy!"

"It ought to be good," he replied, "it has been the work of many generations."

"And then you have added so much to it yourself, you are always buying books."

"I cannot comprehend the neglect of a family library in such days as these."

JANE AUSTEN
Pride and Prejudice

In my teens I spent a lot of time at the new public library. My aunt patronized the private lending library at Boots the Chemist, but growing curious about my library, she followed me there and was dazzled by what she saw and, like many middle-class people round the country, became a convert to the public library system. Being cautious, she would lightly roast the books in our oven for the sake of the germs.

MICHAEL HOLROYD

Come, and take a choice of all my library;
And so beguile thy sorrow.

WILLIAM SHAKESPEARE

News item:

Seventy-year-old Eleanor Barry of Long Island, New York was a long-time collector of books, newspapers, and magazines. Police were summoned to her house in December of 1977 when her neighbors reported that they had not seen her for several weeks. When they entered the house, the police found it full of floor to ceiling stacks of books. They had to use an axe to break down her bedroom door because a collapsed stack of books blocked it. Faint cries for help led them to an enormous stack of heavy books which had fallen onto the bed and trapped her there. They were, with some effort, able to rescue her from the pile of books, but unfortunately she died on the way to the hospital, killed by her book collection.

My box has at last arrived. My books! I cannot tell you what they are to me—silent, wealthy, loyal, lovers. I do thank God for my books with every fiber of my being...I see them all just at my elbow now—Plato, Wordsworth, Myers, Bradley, Halburton, St. Augustine, Browning, Tennyson, Amiel and the others.

OSWALD CHAMBERS

I go into my library, and all history unrolls before me. I breathe the morning air of the world while the scent of Eden's roses yet lingered in it, while it vibrated only to the world's first brood of nightingales, and to the laugh of Eve. I see the pyramids building; I hear the shouting of the armies of Alexander.

ALEXANDER SMITH

An unread man has only to read a very few of the great representative novels to find where he stands, what his tastes are likely to be, and what it is that he is looking for in books. A living library is not to be deliberately made. You cannot plan it out on paper and then buy it en bloc. Of course you can make a collection of books in that way, but a collection of books is not a library. A bookstore is a collection of books, but it is not a library. A library is an organism developing side by side with the mind and character of its owner. It is the house of his spirit and is thus furnished progressively in accordance with the progress of his mental life.

RICHARD LE GALLIENNE

The home of any serious desultory reader has to be a shambles of odd reading matter, chiefly because such a reader has no useful principle of exclusion. By the very nature of his reading, his interests tend to widen not to narrow, to exfoliate endlessly, like a magical rose.

JOSEPH EPSTEIN

The foundation of her knowledge was really laid in the idleness of her grandmother's house, where, as most of the other inmates were not reading people, she had uncontrolled use of a library full of books with frontispieces, which she used to climb upon a chair to take down. When she had found one to her taste—she was guided in the selection chiefly by the frontispieces—she carried it into a mysterious apartment which lay beyond the library and which was called, traditionally, no one knew why, the office. Whose office it had been and at what period it had flourished, she never learned; it was enough for her that it contained an echo and a pleasant musty smell and that it was a chamber of disgrace for old pieces of furniture whose infirmities were not always apparent (so that the disgrace seemed unmerited and rendered them victims of injustice) and with which, in the manner of children, she had established relations almost human, certainly dramatic. There was an old haircloth sofa in especial, to which she had confided a hundred childish sorrows. The place owed much of its mysterious melancholy to the fact that it was properly entered from the second door of the house, the door that had been condemned, and that it was secured by bolts which a particularly slender little girl found it impossible to slide. She knew that this silent, motionless portal opened into the street; if the sidelights had not been filled with green paper she might have looked out upon the little brown stoop and the well-worn brick pavement. But she had no wish to look out, for this would have interfered with her theory that there was a strange, unseen place on the other side—a place which became to the child's imagination, according to its different moods, a region of delight of terror....

A crude, cold rain fell heavily; the spring-time was indeed an appeal—and it seemed a cynical, insincere appeal—to patience. Isabel, however, gave as little heed as possible to cosmic treacheries; she kept her eyes on her book and tried to fix her mind. It had lately occurred to her that her mind was a good deal of a vagabond, and she had spent much ingenuity in training it to a military step and teaching it to advance, to halt, to retreat, to perform even more complicated maneuvers, at the word of command.

HENRY JAMES
Portrait of a Lady

I suspect that the real attraction was a large library of fine books, which was left to dust and spiders since Uncle March died. Jo remembered the kind old gentleman, who used to let her build railroads and bridges with his big dictionaries, tell her stories about the queer pictures in his Latin books, and buy her cards of ginger-bread whenever he met her in the street. The dim, dusty room, with the busts staring down from the tall book-cases, the cozy chairs, the globes, and, best of all, the wilderness of books, in which she could wander where she liked, made the library a region of bliss to her. The moment Aunt March took her nap, or was busy with company, Jo hurried to this quiet place, and, curling her-self up in the easy-chair, devoured poetry, romance, history, travels, and pictures, like a regular book-worm. But, like all happiness, it did not last long; for as sure as she had just reached the heart of the story, the sweetest verse of the song, or the most perilous adventure of her traveler, a shrill voice called, "Josy-phine! Josy-phine!" and she had to leave her paradise to wind yarn, wash the poodle, or read Belsham's Essays *by the hour together.*

LOUISA MAY ALCOTT
Little Women

A library is true fairyland, a very palace of delight, a haven of repose from the storms and troubles of the world. Rich and poor can enjoy it alike, for here, at least, wealth gives no advantage.

AVEBURY

Once I lived in a city, where books bright and pretty
Were ranged in a long shining row on the shelf.
I'd an exquisite cover, gilt-lettered all over,
And not one was more beautiful than myself.

My next place of dwelling—I blush at the telling—
Was a schoolroom as dusty as dusty could be,
Where long I was studied, scratched, thumb-marked
and muddied,
And ruined as any one plainly can see.

And here I am lying, degraded and dying,
While old dusty cobwebs are covering me o'er,
Alone and forsaken, while naught can awaken
The glory I knew in the sweet days of yore.

LILLIE SHELDON

CHAPTER 6

HAPPINESS IS A BOUND BOOK

In a recent conversation, a friend who I regard as generally well-informed paused a minute and measured his words before finally waving his hand toward one of the many bookcases that line the walls of nearly every room in my house and saying, "Before long, computer technology will make books obsolete." He must have glimpsed my horrified reaction, because he quickly demurred, "Don't you think?"

Of course, I knew what he had in mind. He was considering the advantages of storing texts electronically rather than in bulky volumes between covers. Certainly, whole libraries worth of information could be stored on a handful of CD roms. Or books could be placed on the Internet, where they could be downloaded at will.

But replace the book? Certainly not. The very advantages of this new technology are also its disadvantages.

Simply put, you cannot easily climb into bed and read from a computer. But with a book, you can savor the last moments of the day. Then with the gentle onrush of sleep, the book drops lazily to your side, to be retrieved in the morning. And you can't take a computer into the tub, to languidly pass an hour with it precariously poised in one hand above the surface of the water while your skin begins to wrinkle.

No, the book will never be replaced by the computer.

The book is ever ready. It doesn't need to be booted up, and you don't need to search through a hierarchy of files in quest of what you want to read. A canceled check, a coupon, or a scrap of paper torn from the daily news will all serve equally well to mark the spot you discontinued your reading. Some even choose to turn down the corners of the

Often I sat up in my room reading the greatest part of the night, when the book was borrowed in the evening and to be returned early in the morning, lest it should be missed or wanted.

BENJAMIN FRANKLIN

page, not only marking their present location in the book but also leaving a visible record of their progress through it.

A book shows the marks of its interaction with human beings. Pages become stained with coffee or tea and smudged with our fingerprints. Some of the pages show wear from frequent visits at favorite passages. Crumbs slip down into the space between the pages. We mark or highlight thoughts which strike us, scribble agreement or dissent in the margins. Over time, a cherished book takes on characteristics of its owner.

> ***Never read a book through merely because you have begun it.***
> JOHN WITHERSPOON

There is also something of permanence about the printed book, the ink indelibly stained onto the page. The letters join to form words and sentences that will be present for

generations. The words on a computer screen, on the other hand, are only flickering ghosts. They are ephemeral, with no existence outside the mathematics of a series of electrical impulses. They are temporary, removable at a keystroke.

A book is a physical reality. It has a history. When I hold a book in my hands, I hold memories. I can pluck a book off my shelf and cradle it in my hands while I remember the circumstances of my life during the time I first read it. Memories of lost loves, of philosophical breakthroughs, of pains both great and small are intertwined with the plots and characters of novels read during that passage of my life. The books on my shelves beckon me, eagerly waiting to be read.

No, the computer will never replace the book.

Despite his off-the-mark statement, I still cherish a close friendship with my technological friend. But I have learned to be cautious about his judgments.

After all, how could anybody be so wrong about books?

When I am dead,
I hope it will be said:
His Sins were scarlet,
but his books were read.

HILAIRE BELLOC

Does it afflict you to find your books wearing out? I mean literally...The mortality of inanimate things is terrible to me, but that of books most of all.

WILLIAM DEAN HOWELLS

The three practical rules, then, which I have to offer, are:

1. Never read any book that is not a year old.

2. Never read any but famed books.

3. Never read any but what you like.

RALPH WALDO EMERSON

The man who does not read good books has no advantage over the man who can't read them.

MARK TWAIN

The way a book is read—which is to say, the qualities a reader brings to a book—can have as much to do with its worth as anything the author puts into it...Anyone who can read can learn how to read deeply and thus live more fully.

NORMAN COUSINS

They [books] support us in solitude....They help us to forget the coarseness of men and things, compose our cares and our passions, and lay our disappointments to sleep.

STEPHANIE FELICITE GENLIS

Every man who knows how to read has it in his power to magnify himself, to multiply the ways in which he exists, to make his life full, significant and interesting.

ALDOUS HUXLEY

Hence, while Marilla and Mrs. Rachel were enjoying themselves hugely at the mass meeting, Anne and Matthew had the cheerful kitchen at Green Gables all to themselves. A bright fire was glowing in the old-fashioned Waterloo stove and blue-white frost crystals were shining on the windowpanes. Matthew nodded over a Farmers' Advocate *on the sofa and Anne at the table studied her lessons with grim determination, despite sundry wistful glances at the clock shelf, where lay a new book that Jane Andrews had lent her that day. Jane had assured her that it was warranted to produce any number of thrills, or words to that effect, and Anne's fingers tingled to reach out for it. But that would mean Gilbert Blythe's triumph on the morrow. Anne turned her back on the clock shelf and tried to imagine it wasn't there.*

LUCY MAUD MONTGOMERY

Anne of Green Gables

A saw-mill run by water power consists of a shed built on the bank of a stream. The roof is supported by a framework resting on four large wooden posts. At a height of eight or ten feet, in the middle of the shed, is the saw swaying up and down, while a very simple contrivance pushes the logs before it. A wheel turned by the water produces both these movements—that of the saw sliding up and down, and that by which the logs are slowly brought in front of it.

Approaching his mill, old Sorel, in stentorian tones, called for Julien. No one answered. He could only see his eldest sons, a race of giants, trimming fir logs with their heavy axes. They were intently following the black lines traced over the logs; with each stroke of the axe immense slivers were falling away. They did not hear their father's voice. The latter therefore walked toward the shed. When he entered, he looked in vain for Julien, who should have been at work by the saw. He observed him five or six feet higher up, astride a beam beneath the roof. Instead of tending to the machinery, Julien was reading. Nothing was so exasperating to old Sorel. He could have forgiven Julien his slight figure, which was so ill-adapted to heavy work, and was so different from his elder sons; but this mania for reading he despised—he himself did not know how to read.

He called Julien two or three times, but in vain. The attention he was giving to the book, more than the noise of the machinery, prevented him from hearing anything. The latter, then, in spite of his age, leaped lightly upon the shaft supporting the framework of the saw, and from there to the horizontal beam beneath the roof. A violent blow sent into the river the book Julien was holding; a second one, equally violent, aimed at his head, made him lose his balance. He was about to fall twelve or fifteen feet below, on top of the moving machinery, where he would have been crushed, when his father caught him with his left hand as he slipped.

"Now, you lazy good-for-nothing! So you'll then always be reading your damned books when you should be minding the saw? Read them at night when you go to waste your time at the curate's!"

Julien, though stunned by the blow, and bleeding, went to his post of duty by the saw. There were tears in his eyes, less from physical pain than from the loss of the book he loved.

STENDAHL
The Red and the Black

Books become as familiar and necessary as old friends. Each change in them, brought about by much handling and by accident only endears them more. They are an extension of oneself.

CHARLOTTE GRAY

The love of reading enables a man to exchange the wearisome hours of life, which come to every one, for hours of delight.

MONTESQUIEU

These "Laws of Caring for Books" composed by a medieval German Rabbi demonstrate once again how highly the printed page was esteemed among the Jews:

Nor shall a man write any accounts upon the pages of a book or scribble anything on any part of it.

One must be careful not to keep his books in the same receptacle with food, for fear of the mice nibbling them both.

If one is unable to press the leaves of a book together in order to fasten the clasp, he shall not place his knees upon it to force it to close.

If a father dies, and leaves a dog and a book to his sons, one of the children shall not say to the other, "You take the dog and I'll have the book," for what a disgraceful contrast are these two objects!

If one wishes to take a nap, he must first cover his books up, and not recline upon them.

If a book has fallen to the ground, and at the same time some money or a sumptuous garment has fallen also, he shall first pick up the book. If a fire breaks out in his house, he shall first rescue his books, and then his other property. Nor shall he ever think the time spent upon attending to books wasted; and even if he finds a book so full of errors as that correction of them would be useless, he shall not destroy the book, but place it in some out-of-the-way corner.

A man is obliged to be very careful as to the respect due to books, for by not acting thus he is behaving offensively to his fellow-man, whose brain has produced these books.

RABBI JUDAHBEN SAMUEL SIR LEON CHÀSSID

A precious mouldering pleasure 'tis
To meet an antique book
In just the dress his century wore;
A privilege, I think,

His venerable hand to take,
A warming in our own,
A passage back, or two, to make
To times when he was young.

His quaint opinions to inspect,
His knowledge to unfold
On what concerns our mutual mind,
The literature of old:

What impressed the scholars most,
What competitions ran
When Plato was a certainty
And Sophocles a man,

When Sappho was a living girl,
And Beatrice wore
The gown that Dante deified.
Facts, centuries before,

He traverses familiar,
As one should come to town
And tell you all your dreams were true:
He lived where dreams are sown.

His presence is enchantment,
You beg him not to go;
His volumes shake their vellum heads
And tantalize, just so.

EMILY DICKINSON

CHAPTER 7

FRIENDS FOR LIFE

ecently a friend made a confession to me.

For years he had found himself obsessed with an unattainable woman. He knew that the two of them would never be able to be together; it was hopeless, impossible. And yet she continued to weigh on his mind, always lurking there just on the outskirts of his consciousness, often emerging as the focus of dreamlike musings.

He had first met her when he was still a teenager, and even at that early age he knew that she was the summation of all he desired. He also knew she was out of his reach. For months after meeting her, she was all he could think of. He found himself, even now, years later, thinking about her at unexpected moments. She had remained for him the standard by which every other woman was judged. It was foolish, he knew. It could never be. Still, she was a permanent part of his thoughts. And he always wanted to hold her there.

Her name was Jane...Jane Eyre.

And though she had no material substance, existing only in the printed pages of Charlotte Bronte's novel, how real she was in his heart and mind.

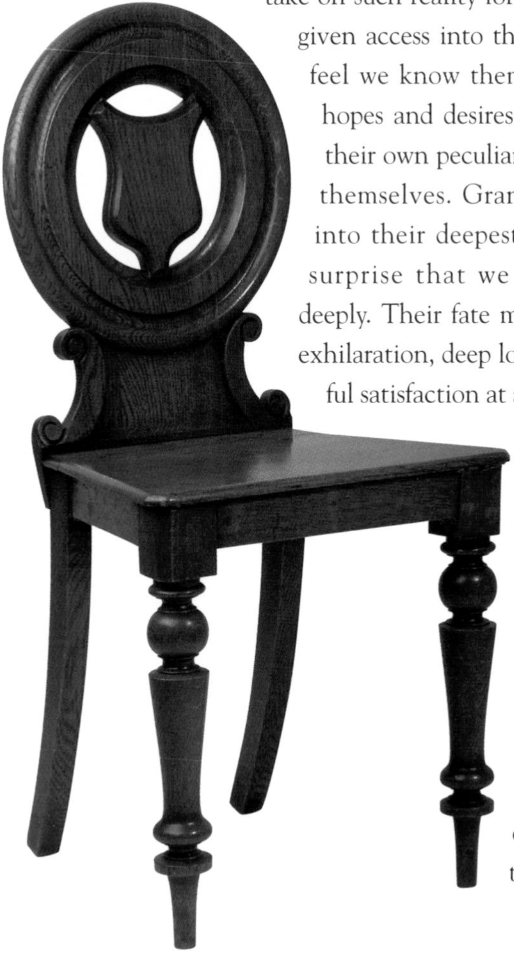

Characters from favorite stories will always take on such reality for us. Because we are given access into their interior life, we feel we know them intimately: their hopes and desires, fears and failures, their own peculiar view of life and of themselves. Granted this entrance into their deepest musings, it is no surprise that we come to care so deeply. Their fate moves us to tears or exhilaration, deep longing or a wonderful satisfaction at a happy ending.

Aristotle taught that art provides a catharsis, an emotional cleansing and purification as our emotions are exercised in feeling compassion for the figures in the unfolding drama. We fear for their safety, mourn over their losses, worry over their downturns of fortune, and exult over their successes in love and life. Sometimes a whole extra lifetime's worth of experiences are offered to us in a good book. Our own range of feelings are expanded as we spend time with our literary friends.

Who could, once having read of them, forget the proud but virtuous Mr. Darcy, the tragically foolish Emma Bovary, the misunderstood Jean Valjean, the loyal Hester Prynne, the saintly Alyosha Karamazov, the meddling but well-intentioned Emma Woodhouse, or the worldly-wise Tom Sawyer? Are they not as real as many of our acquaintances?

Of course, the people we meet in books are not always fictional. Historical characters can also leap out of the pages of biographies or history books to take on a reality of their own. My wife testifies that a childhood reading of a biography of Therese de Liseux, the beloved nun who has come to be called "the little flower," changed the direction of her life. After meeting Therese in the pages of a book, she set out to emulate the nun's saintly simplicity, not by becoming a nun herself, but by holding Therese's example of sanctity before her mind. She found herself asking how Therese might respond to the kind of pressures and temptations that came to her in her own life. Another friend has said that Amy Carmichael's life story affected her in a similar way.

The first time I read an excellent book, it is to me just as if I had gained a new friend. When I read over a book I have perused before, it resembles the meeting with an old one.

OLIVER GOLDSMITH

Was my friend who was so enamored with Jane Eyre just a little too obsessed? Was he in need of some psychiatric help in separating fantasy from reality? I don't think so. Deep down, he really had been powerfully touched by her. She was his ideal.

And who could argue with his choice?

I never remain passive in the process of reading: while I read I am engaged in a constant creative activity, which leads me to remember not so much the actual matter of the book as the thoughts evoked in my mind by it, directly or indirectly.

NICOLAS BERDYAEV

In a very real sense, people who have read good literature have lived more than people who cannot or will not read... It is not true that we can have only one life to live; if we can read, we can live as many more lives and as many kinds of lives as we wish.

S. I. HAYAKAWA

Books are delightful when prosperity happily smiles; when adversity threatens, they are inseparable comforters. They give strength to human compacts, nor are grave opinions brought forward without books. Arts and sciences, the benefits of which no mind can calculate, depend upon books.

RICHARD DE BURY

Friends, books, a cheerful heart, and conscience clear
Are the most choice companions we have here.

WILLIAM MATHER

Dreams, books, are each a world, and books we know,
Are a substantial world, both pure and good.
Round these, with tendrils strong as flesh and blood,
Our pastime and our happiness will grow.

WILLIAM WORDSWORTH

"My wife doesn't care about gardening," said Charles, "although she has been advised to take exercise, she prefers always sitting in her room reading."

"Like me," replied Léon. "And indeed, what is better than to sit by one's fireside in the evening with a book, while the wind beats against the window and the lamp is burning?"

"What indeed?" she said, fixing her large black eyes wide open upon him.

"One thinks of nothing," he continued; "the hours slip by. Motionless we traverse countries we fancy we see, and your thought, blending with the fiction, playing with the details, follows the outline of the adventures. It mingles with the characters, and it seems as if it were yourself palpitating beneath their costumes."

"That is true! that is true!" she said.

"Has it ever happened to you," Léon went on, "to come across some vague idea of one's own in a book, some dim image that comes back to you from afar, and as the completest expression of your own slightest sentiment?"

"I have experienced it," she replied.

"That is why," he said, "I especially love the poets. I think verse more tender than prose, and that it moves far more easily to tears."

"Still in the long-run it is tiring," continued Emma. "Now I, on the contrary, adore stories that rush breathlessly along, that frighten one. I detest

commonplace heroes and moderate sentiments, such as there are in nature."

"In fact," observed the clerk, "these works, not touching the heart, miss, it seems to me, the true end of art. It is so sweet, amid all the disenchantments of life, to be able to swell in thought upon noble characters, pure affections, and pictures of happiness. For myself, living here far from the world, this is my one distraction; but Yonville affords so few resources."

"Like Tostes, no doubt," replied Emma; "and so I always subscribed to a lending library."

GUSTAVE FLAUBERT
Madame Bovary

While you converse with lords and dukes,
I have their betters here—my books.

THOMAS SHERIDAN

Oh! but books are such safe company! They keep your Secrets well; they never boast they made your eyes glisten, or your cheek flush, or your heart throb. You may take up your favorite Author, and love him at a distance just as warmly as you like, for all the sweet fancies and glowing thoughts that have winged your lonely hours so fleetly and so sweetly. Then you may close the book, and lean your cheek against the cover, as if it were the face of a dear friend; shut your eyes and soliloquize to your heart's content, without fear of misconstruction...You may put the volume under your pillow, and let your eye and the first ray of morning light fall on it together, and nothing shall rob you of that delicious pleasure. You may have a thousand petty, provoking, irritating annoyances through the day, and you shall come back to your dear old book, and forget them all in dreamland. It shall be a friend that shall be always at hand; that shall never try you by caprice, or pain you by forgetfulness, or wound you by distrust.

SARA P. PARTON

It is very difficult for a man who has fallen in love with Rosalind and Heloise, Emma and the Duchess of Malfi, to settle for someone merely alive. And where is a woman to find a Sir Lancelot?

MAYA V. PATEL

It is a sign of intimacy to be able to read in the same room with another person, as trusting as dreaming with someone right beside you.

LAURA FURMAN/ELINORE STANDARD

My best friend is a person who will give me a book I have not read.

ABRAHAM LINCOLN

We use books like mirrors, gazing into them only to discover ourselves.

JOSEPH EPSTEIN

A truly great book should be read in youth, again in maturity, and once more in old age.

ROBERTSON DAVIES

Every night, after supper, we read some part of a small collection of romances which had been my mother's. My father's design was only to improve me in reading, and he thought these entertaining works were calculated to give me a fondness for it; but we soon found ourselves so interested in the adventures they contained, that we alternately read whole nights together, and could not bear to give over until at the conclusion of a volume. Sometimes, in a morning, on hearing the swallows at our window, my father, quite ashamed of this weakness, would cry, "Come, come, let us go to bed; I am more a child than thou art."

I soon acquired, by this dangerous custom, not only an extreme facility in reading and comprehending, but, for my age, a too intimate acquaintance with the passions. An infinity of sensations were familiar to me, without possessing any precise idea of the objects to which they related—I had conceived nothing—I had felt the whole. This confused succession of emotions did not retard the future efforts of my reason, though they added an extravagant, romantic notion of human life, which experience and reflection have never been able to eradicate.

JEAN JACQUES ROUSSEAU

Confessions

CHAPTER 8

BOOKS AS SPIRITUAL COMPANIONS

Life can be confusing. Daily, we face crossroads that call for important choices about the direction of our lives: Where am I going? Which pathways should I travel? What kind of person do I want to become? These questions can be very vexing for we know that many of our daily choices will have long-term consequences further down the road. Indeed, life is a journey.

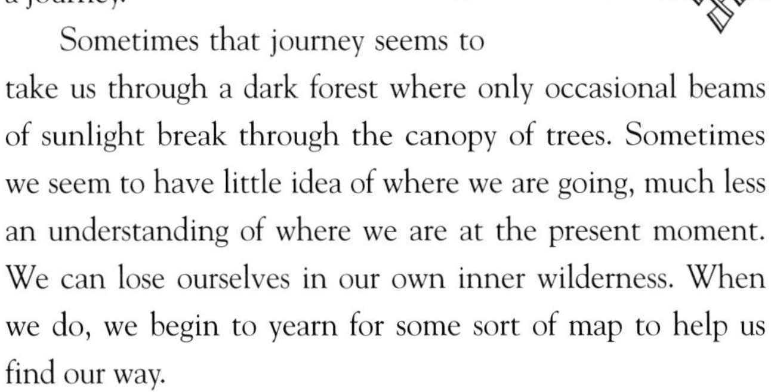

Sometimes that journey seems to take us through a dark forest where only occasional beams of sunlight break through the canopy of trees. Sometimes we seem to have little idea of where we are going, much less an understanding of where we are at the present moment. We can lose ourselves in our own inner wilderness. When we do, we begin to yearn for some sort of map to help us find our way.

Books provide the most helpful of road maps for this inner journey. They show us the tracks of fellow travelers, footprints left by earlier pilgrims who have trod the path that stretches before us. Their luminosity helps to light our way. As we read we realize that we are not alone.

> *How many a man has dated a new era in his life from the reading of a book!*
> HENRY DAVID THOREAU

Buried in the pages of books we find experiences and thoughts that are similar to our own, yet crystallized for us, phrased in a way we could never frame with our own fumbling words. Sometimes we realize with a start: Someone else knows! Someone we have never known, someone possibly long dead, becomes now a valued comrade. We walk the path just behind this someone, eyes alert for light in our present darkness. We sense a communion with such writers. They become our teachers and friends.

The books they write are patient companions. They do not rush us or press themselves upon us with opportunity. Rather, they wait for us to come to them. They seem to understand that eternal matters are not settled in a day. The journey of life is not taken as the crow flies, but is made up of the twisting turns of a country mile. Sometimes, just around the bend, a book is waiting that will be exactly what we need.

That's why a well-chosen book can make such a perfect gift for a friend, a fellow pilgrim. The right book placed in the right hands at the right time can make a lasting difference. Few other gifts can make that claim. When was the last time you received a tie that changed your life?

Without the influence of books in my life, I fear I would have missed so much…

…so much beauty. Consider the poets, who catch the fleeting glories of the moment, who disimprison the wonder that lies all about us. Their simple words give us new eyes to see. They frame the ordinary with a radiance we so often miss in the rush of living our lives, like the shimmer of eternity in the fragile loveliness of a rose.

…so much joy. I think of the novelists, who evoke laughter from the comedy of life, the breathless bewilderment of love found, or the depleted hollowness of love lost. Their words summon the remembrance of things past and feelings long buried by our pains and forgetfulness. Their stories remind us that though life is never easy, each tragedy can somehow be a victory, an overcoming that gives evidence of the triumph of the human spirit.

...so much truth. Beauty and joy are meaningless if they are the result of living in an illusion. Philosophers and contemplatives, scientists and saints—they have sought to distill our human experiences and make sense of them. And they have paid a price for this pursuit of truth. They have been misunderstood, misquoted, or made an outcast. Yet in books their words survive the onslaughts of fashion and of time to reach out to us over the chasm of years. They offer a hand to lift us and light to guide us. They point us to the One who is the Light, the One in whom truth, beauty, and joy dance in concert to the music of the spheres. The stars sing his name.

Countless are those who have walked beside me, writers to whom I owe a debt of gratitude. They have helped me move closer to an understanding of myself, given me glimpses of the reality of God, helped me shed my misperceptions, and offered a handhold when I felt I was falling.

I would not want to be without books.

Which is the real possessor of a book—the man who has its original and every following edition, and shows, to many an admiring and envying visitor, now this, now that, in binding characteristic, with possessor-pride...or the man who cherishes one little, hollow-backed, coverless, untitled, bethumbed copy, which he takes with him in his solitary walks and broods over in his silent chamber, always finding in it some beauty or excellence or aid he had not found before—which is to him in truth as a live companion?

GEORGE MACDONALD

It is chiefly through books that we enjoy intercourse with superior minds...In the best books, great men talk to us, give us their most precious thoughts, and pour their souls into ours.

WILLIAM ELLERY CHANNING

If he shall not lose his reward who gives a cup of cold water to his thirsty neighbor, what will not be the reward of those who by putting good books into the hands of those neighbors, open to them the fountains of eternal life?

THOMAS À KEMPIS

A book is like a garden carried in the pocket.

CHINESE PROVERB

A book must be an ice-ax to break the seas frozen in our souls.

FRANZ KAFKA

Books are the compass and telescopes and sextants and charts which other men have prepared to help us navigate the dangerous seas of human life.

JESSE LEE BENNETT

Reading is to the mind what exercise is to the body. As by the one, health is preserved, strengthened, and invigorated; by the other, virtue (which is the health of the mind) is kept alive, cherished, and confirmed.

JOSEPH ADDISON

Reading books in one's youth is like looking at the moon through a crevice; reading books in middle age is like looking at the moon in one's courtyard; and reading books in old age is like looking at the moon on an open terrace. This is because the depth of benefits of reading varies in proportion to the depth of one's own experience.

CHANG CH'AO

Of all the inanimate objects, of all men's creations, books are the nearest to us, for they contain our very thoughts, our ambitions, our indignations, our illusions, our fidelity to truth, and our persistent leaning toward error. But most of all they resemble us in the precarious hold on life.

JOSEPH CONRAD

Books—you are wonderful. In you live the hope, the comfort, the philosophy, the glory, the peace, the reward of a world. You line the edge of my life. As I view you—of a thousand lives expressed and of a hundred thousand thoughts revealed—I say that come what may, so long as I stick to you, I shall not be entirely alone.

GEORGE MATTHEW ADAMS

Books are the quietest and most constant friends; they are the most accessible and wisest of counsellors, and the most patient of teachers.

CHARLES W. ELIOT

Except a living man there is nothing more wonderful than a book!—a message to us from the dead—from human souls we never saw, and who lived perhaps thousands of miles away; and yet these words on those little sheets of paper speak to us, amuse us, and comfort us.

CHARLES KINGSLEY

The reading of all good books is like a conversation with the finest men of past centuries.

RENÉ DESCARTES

Some books are meant to be tasted, others to be swallowed, and some few to be chewed and digested; that is, some books are to be read only in parts; others to be read but not curiously; and some few to be read wholly, and with diligence and attention.

FRANCIS BACON

These are not books, lumps of lifeless paper, but minds alive on the shelves. From each of them goes out its own voice…and just as the touch of a button on our set will fill the room with music, so by taking down one of these volumes and opening it, one can call into range the voice of a man far distant in time and space and hear him speaking to us, mind to mind, heart to heart.

GILBERT HIGHET

That is part of the beauty of all literature. You discover that your longings are universal longings, that you're not alone and isolated from anyone. You belong.

F. SCOTT FITZGERALD

A book is good company. It comes to your longing with full instruction, but pursues you never. It is not offended at your absent-mindedness, nor jealous if you turn to other pleasures, of leaf, or dress, or mineral, or even of books. It silently serves the soul without recompense, not even for the hire of love. And yet more noble, it seems to pass from itself, and to enter the memory, and to hover in a silvery transformation there, until the outward book is but a body and its soul and spirit are flown to you, and possess your memory like a spirit.

HENRY WARD BEECHER

The collaboration between the book and the reader is intimate, private. We must not forget that pleasure, discretion, silence, and creative solitude are the primary characteristics of a life of reading; its most tangible justification and most immediate reward. Solitude may appear now to be an unaffordable luxury, yet any book creates for the reader a place elsewhere. A person reading is a person suspended between the immediate and the timeless. This suspension serves a purpose that has little to do with escaping from the real world, the sin avid readers are most commonly accused of.

VARTAN GREGORIAN

Every book is, in an intimate sense, a circular letter to the friends of him who writes it.

ROBERT LOUIS STEVENSON

Books may preach when the author cannot, when the author may not, when the author dares not, yea, and which is more, when the author is not.

THOMAS BROOKS

Then alter not, O book, fulfil your destiny.
You are not a reminiscence of the land alone.
You too as a lone bark cleaving the ether, purpos'd
I know not whither, yet ever full of faith.

WALT WHITMAN

He ate and drank the previous Words—
His spirit grew robust—
He knew no more that he was poor,
Nor that his frame was Dust—

He danced along the dingy Days
And this Bequest of Wings
Was but a Book—What Liberty
A loosened spirit brings—

EMILY DICKINSON

At last Maggie's eyes glanced down on the books that lay on the window-shelf, and she half forsook her reverie to turn over listlessly the leaves of the Portrait Gallery, *but she soon pushed this aside to examine the little row of books tied together with string.* Beauties of the Spectator, Rasselas, Economy of Human Life, Gregory's Letter—*she knew the sort of matter that was inside all these; the* Christian Year—*that seemed to be a hymn book, and she laid it down again; but Thomas à Kempis?—the name had come across her in her reading, and she felt the satisfaction, which everyone knows, of getting some ideas to attach to a name that strays solitary in the memory. She took up the little, old, clumsy book with some curiosity; it had the corners turned down in many places, and some hand, now forever quiet, had made at certain passages strong pen and ink marks, long since browned by time.*

She read on and on in the old book, devouring eagerly the dialogues with the invisible Teacher, the pattern of sorrow, the source of strength; returning to it after she had been called away, and reading till the sun went down behind the willows.

She knew nothing of doctrines and systems—of mysticism or quietism but this voice out of the far-off middle ages was the direct communication of a human soul's belief and experience, and came to Maggie as an unquestioned message.

I suppose that is the reason why the small old-fashioned book, for which you need only pay six-pence at a bookstall, works miracles to this day, turning bitter waters into sweetness: while expensive sermons and treatises, newly issued, leave all things as they were before. It was written down by a hand that waited for the heart's prompting; it is the chronicle of a solitary, hidden anguish, struggle, trust and triumph...It remains to all time a lasting record of human needs and human consolations: the voice of a brother who, ages ago, felt and suffered and renounced—in the cloister, perhaps with serge gown and tonsured head, with much chanting and long fasts, and with a fashion of speech different from ours—but under the same silent, far-off heavens, and with the same passionate desires, the same strivings, the same failures, the same weariness.

GEORGE ELIOT
The Mill on the Floss

Only three things are necessary to make life happy: the blessing of God, books, and a friend.

LACORDAIRE

The peace of great books be for you,

Stains of pressed clover leaves on pages,

Bleach of the light of years held in leather.

CARL SANDBURG

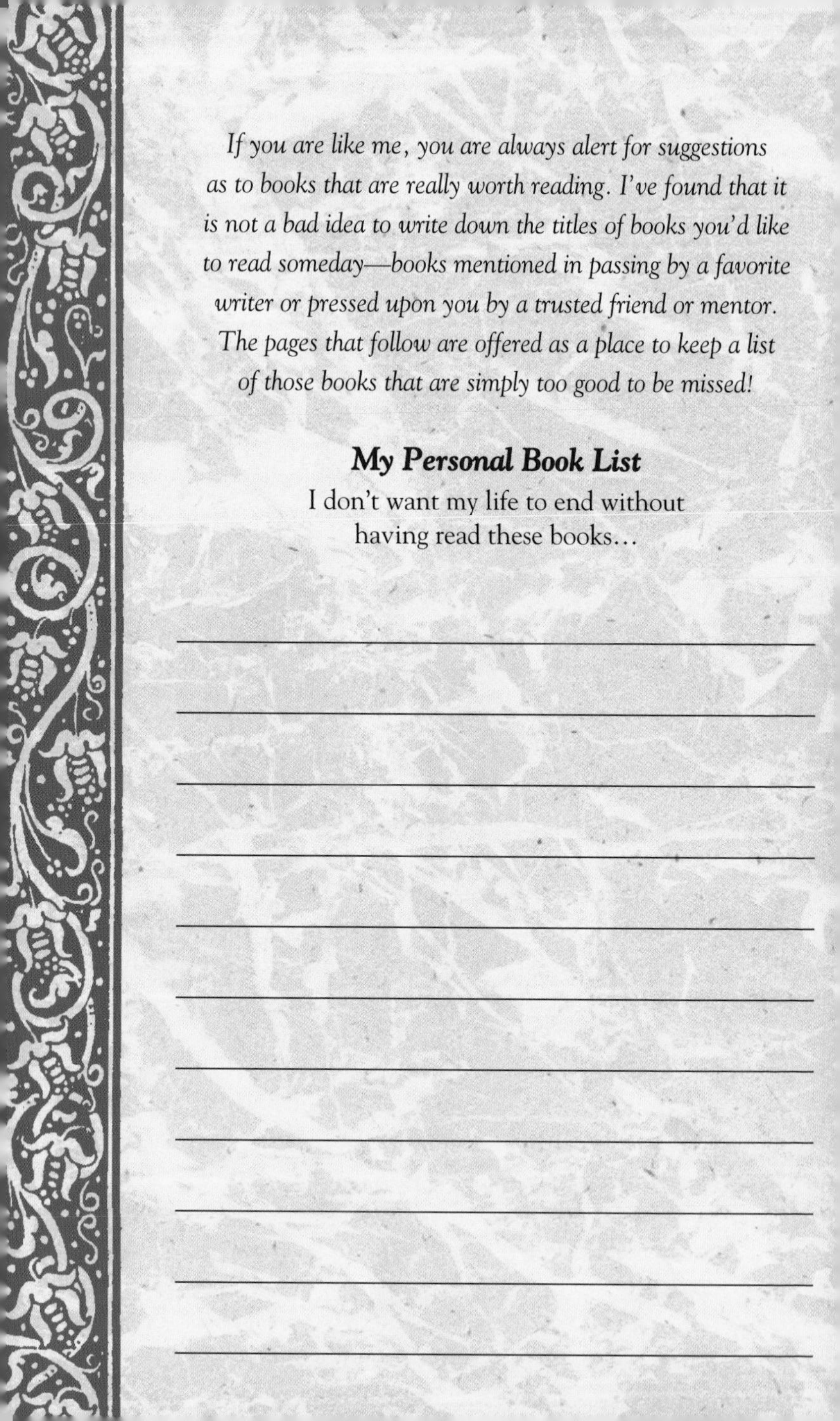

If you are like me, you are always alert for suggestions as to books that are really worth reading. I've found that it is not a bad idea to write down the titles of books you'd like to read someday—books mentioned in passing by a favorite writer or pressed upon you by a trusted friend or mentor. The pages that follow are offered as a place to keep a list of those books that are simply too good to be missed!

My Personal Book List

I don't want my life to end without having read these books…

Art Credits

Julius Melchers, *The Sun Porch*, Peter Harboldt, SuperStock.

Silvestro Lega, *Grandmother's Lesson*, Municipal Palace Peschieva des Garde, SuperStock, London.

Seymour Guy, *Knowledge Is Power*, Christie's Images / SuperStock.

Tissot, *Reading a Book*, Christie's Images, London / Bridgeman Art Library, London / SuperStock.

Kamir, *Femme Lisant* (Woman Reading), Musee d'Disay, Paris / Giraudon, Paris / SuperStock.

Martha Walter, *Young Boy in White Reading Book*, David David Gallery, Philadelphia / SuperStock.

Monet, *La Liseuse* (The Reader), Walters Art Gallery, Baltimore / Lauros-Giraudon, Paris / SuperStock.

Renoir, *Fisher with Rod and Line*, Private Collection / Bridgeman Art Library, London / SuperStock.

Mary Cassat, *Family Group Reading*, Philadelphia Museum of Art / SuperStock.

Gebhardt, *The Students*, SuperStock.

Fischer, *The Afternoon Read*, Christie's Images / SuperStock.

Spiteweg, *The Bookworm*, Schweinfurt, Collection of Dr. G. Schafer / A.K.G., Berlin / SuperStock.

Hans Heyerdahl, *At the Window*, National Gallery, Oslo, Norway / Bridgeman Art Library, London / SuperStock.

Sir James Shannon, *On the Dunes*, Art Rersource, New York.

Eastman Johnson, *The Girl I Left Behind Me*, National Musuem of American Art, Washington D.C. / Art Resource.

Ilya Repin, *Tolstoy Reading in Woods*, Tretyakov Gallery, Moscow / Art Resource.

Vittorio Matteo Corcos, *Dreams*, Galleria Nazionale d'Arte Moderna, Rome / Art Resource.

Catherine M. Wood, *Books*, Mallett & Son Antiques Ltd., London / Bridgeman Art Library.

Thomas Rowlandson, *Library of the Royal Institution*, Art Resource.

James Charles Lewis, *Reading by the Window*, Christie's Images / The Bridgeman Art Library.

George Friedrich Kersting, *Man Reading Under a Lamp*, Art Resource.

Cecil Rice, *Comfort & Joy*, Acworth, Georgia.

Acknowledgments

Page 11: From *Charing Cross Road* by Helene Hanff. Copyright ©1970 by Helene Hanff. Used by permission of Viking Penguin, a division of Penguin Putman, Inc.

Page 38: Reprinted by permission of the publisher from *One Writer's Beginnings* by Eudora Welty, Cambridge, Mass.: Harvard University Press, Copyright ©1983, 1984 by Eudora Welty.

Page 107: From *Smoke and Steel* by Carl Sandburg. Used by permission of Harcourt Brace & Company.